MW01531367

Grace Garden

A HARVEST OF LIFE LESSONS

Rod Giles

Grace Garden

A HARVEST OF LIFE LESSONS

Rod Giles

STORIA PUBLISHING

TULSA, OKLAHOMA
STORIAWRITER.COM

Book design by Megan Morrow

Original artwork by Tammie O'Neal

tammieoneal.com

ISBN 979-8-9857364-9-6

Printed in the United States of America

Storia Editing and Publishing, LLC

storiawriter.com

Table of Contents

Grace Garden

Preface

I remember my mother tending her garden back home in the upper Midwest. She was a member and leader in the Fort Dodge, Iowa, garden club and got many of her ideas from friends who shared her interest in cutting flower arrangements. Tulips and irises were her flowers of choice.

My mother was a very refined and traditional gardener.

As a young boy, my understanding of gardening was shaped by growing up in the middle of a wild and wonderful forested city park. Crawford Park was part of Roosevelt's work projects in the 1930s and is filled with tall cliffs and water running over the stone bridges. I knew Crawford Park like the back of my hand. I climbed Clay Cliff, built rafts and floated them on the creek, and sledded down snow-covered hills in the winter. Later, as a Boy Scout, I learned to camp and live well in the woods. I was in my element. As a camp counselor at Lake Okoboji, I learned even more from the resident camp ranger, Barney, as he was known by campers and Scouters. I taught nature, water, and soil conservation merit badges to Scouts for three wonderful summers in my teen years. During this time, I also grew in my faith in Christ and His creation and developed a deep spiritual connection with nature.

Early on, I decided this book would be more than just a gardening book. My bookshelf is filled with gardening manuals and how-to books with facts and tips. *Grace Garden: A Harvest of Life Lessons* draws on the deeper spiritual connection I feel in the wildness of nature and in a welltended garden. This book is my way of testifying to the world the glory of God's creation.

Introduction

I became a "man of the dirt" during one of the darkest periods of my life. I was recuperating from open heart surgery and enjoying a pity party one day in my backyard. Although I am a person of faith, on that particular day, I was upset with God, life, and everything in between. I remember shaking my fist in the air and shouting, "So, what do you want me to do now?"

The surgery had been months earlier, but I was still unable to do most of the physical activities in the garden. I couldn't walk far without getting winded and light-headed. And in the middle of the smallest activity, I would have to sit on the floor to keep from falling and injuring myself further.

My mind continued to be muddled from anesthesia, and I often found it difficult to put thoughts into words. That was especially scary to me, because, several years earlier, I watched my mother sink into the world of Alzheimer's. I thought this might be the beginning of the end for me. That day, God's answer came quickly: "Just dig." I didn't hear God's voice in my head, but I was sure His Spirit was speaking to my spirit. I had my answer.

As a boy, I learned the names of almost every plant in Crawford Park. In the early spring, I watched with awe as the flowering plant, Helle-bores, would emerge from the forest floor, grow, and bloom. I loved experiencing all four seasons and felt a kinship with everything that grew.

When my spirit heard God say, "Just dig," I knew He wanted me to plant living things, watch them grow, tend them, and create something beautiful. I didn't know much more than that, so I started digging and planting my garden. And I've been digging ever since.

Becoming a man of the dirt has changed the front and back of my yard, but it has also changed my life. Over the last few years, I've realized why I took to the dirt so easily. I am creative and enjoy physical activity. I also love to wander through the plant sections of the big home improvement stores for ideas on plant combinations and how to display them. It's exciting to know that many of those ideas will "take root" in my garden.

In a broader sense, I see real-life lessons in my garden. If you are a gardener, you have probably discovered life lessons of your own. Those of us who are "people of the dirt" have much to tell the next generation. We may even turn them back to the dirt as well.

The best place to seek God is in a garden. You can dig for Him there.

George Bernard Shaw

Chapter 1

A Natural Bent
Toward Anarchy

When left unattended, all things in life move toward entropy, anarchy, and bedlam. In the garden, I call this "botanical chaos." Gardens need borders and boundaries to highlight where the lawn, garden, and other plant groups begin and end. There are many ways to do that: stones, fences, wood chips, and metal edging, to name a few. The goal is practical and visual; you can keep invasive plants from creeping out of their space, and the garden looks all the better.

The garden shrub known as Sumac is a good example. In the fall, the fern-like leaves turn a burnished red, which makes a nice, loose-textured landscape accent. I wanted to create a corner with height and airiness in my garden, so I thought Sumac would be an excellent choice. The result was a disaster. Sumac is extremely invasive and takes over any ground it occupies. Little runners grew everywhere, rapidly overwhelming any border or boundary I put in place. It was not the visual design I was looking for, and that corner of my garden quickly became a nightmare. Cutting it back became time-consuming and laborious. Once I made the decision to choose an alternative, it was already too late. I spent the entire fall season cutting out the Sumac I had planted the year before.

Look at any vacant lot or untilled pasture, and you will see botanical chaos: weeds, grasses, and dead limbs on the ground or hanging from the trees. I have been gardening in my yard for over twelve years, but despite having distinct borders, I am constantly pulling weeds, cutting back shrubs, and trimming vines. If I leave my garden unattended, it takes more time to clean it up and make it beautiful again.

The concept of "botanical chaos" is also true in our personal lives. Boundaries are just as important in life as they are in the garden. The boundaries you set will determine who and what you allow into your life. Many activities we engage in need restrictions and limits, so they don't overwhelm our lives.

We are all gardeners of sorts, tending our "life gardens." We need to say "yes" to some things but "no" to many more. For some of us, pulling out weeds in our lives will require a change in our thinking and habits. For example, we need to weed out those activities that drain us of time and energy with no special payoff. Sometimes, it is simple to do; other times it requires real effort to prune activities and simplify our lives. But it is worth it. When we set and keep boundaries, we increase our satisfaction, productivity, and influence on others. We find satisfaction when we're not tossed about by all of life's choices.

What about your life? How have you chosen what to plant, what to prune, and which weeds to pull?

What kinds of boundaries and borders can you use in your life?

What borders do you need to put in place soon?

Gardening is civil and social, but it wants the vigor and freedom of the forest and the outlaw.

Henry David Thoreau

Chapter 2

Purposeful Pruning Creates Abundant Growth

My most essential garden tools are my pruners, which I have in four different sizes. I use them to cut back shrub growth and to "deadhead" flowers (remove spent blooms). When some of my larger shrubs become bigger, they need cutting back to foster continued growth. If I do nothing, they grow out of control.

As the gardener, I have a plan for every plant in the ground. In the short run, pruning cuts off growth above where you prune. In the long run, it helps shape the plant by redirecting its energy to other areas of growth. Take roses, for example. By cutting off dead or dying flowers, we redirect energy and nutrients to other parts of the plant to grow new buds. On young trees, we trim the lower branches and "trunk up" the overall look of the tree, which helps control the amount of sun and shade in a small area like a garden. This creates a host of mini environments that support different plants and views in the garden. Pruning allows gardeners to create many unique areas within the garden.

Plant growth doesn't take place overnight. Common garden plants may take weeks or months to mature; trees may take years. When using a pruning tool, I'm careful about what I cut. If I snip off the wrong branch or flower top, it can take months or years to re-grow. I have learned the importance of the Latin *phrase primum non nocere*, which means "above all else, do no harm." I adhere to that phrase in my pruning and trimming. I am more conservative in my approach to pruning.

What really hurts is seeing wonderful growth, beautiful foliage, or blossoms growing in the wrong direction. That growth has taken months to develop, but now it requires pruning because the new growth doesn't fit my design plan. As the gardener, I get to choose.

How does all this apply to life, your life, and mine?

Here are a few thoughts:

- Pruning in our lives will come from others, circumstances, and ourselves.
- Pruning is necessary for an orderly life and healthy relationships.
- Sometimes, pruning hurts. Leaving old relationships can be hard.
- Pruning always requires a long-range view.

If you have recently done some pruning in your life, what new growth do you hope will emerge?

What one thing in your life have you thought about pruning? How would that affect the environment of your life's garden?

I am the true vine, and my Father is the gardener. He cuts off every branch in me that bears no fruit, while every branch that does bear fruit, he prunes so that it will be even more fruitful.

The Apostle John (John 15:1)

Chapter 3

A View Toward the Future

One of the most important seasons for my gardening is winter. Planning is critical, and I've found that some tasks should be taken on during certain times, so I garden year-round. In my part of the country, summer gets so hot that I can't work outside as much, and plants grow less because of drought and high heat. Before and after bloom times are often the busiest, and activity may actually pick up in the off-season. During one mild winter, I dug out a small portion of my garden and installed a drain because I wanted that area to grow out during spring and fall.

In late spring, I always walk through the garden to find areas for new daffodil bulbs and other flowers that will bloom in the first weeks of the following spring. I order them early and plant in the fall, but I won't see anything until the following spring.

As the first green sprouts break the earth's surface in early spring, I move plants around to other locations in my garden. Small plants in the back come forward in the beds, and some shrubs are cut back or removed and repositioned. Knowing where plants need to go takes planning. During the growing season, I make mental notes, write in my garden log, or take pictures so I can make changes later.

I look ahead one, two, and even three years, knowing the garden will look different by then. The question is: "What do I have to do today, this month, or this season to bring about the look I want in the future?" Because I plan ahead, I take myself out of the present.

Life is hard, and the present can often be difficult and painful. For those of us with chronic health conditions, it's important to know that the present is not all there is. The expectation of seeing my garden in the coming years helps my mental and physical health and overall well-being. I'm limited in how much I can impact the future; the current situation will change, but I have the opportunity now to affect that change.

As you look toward the future, what one thing can you do today to make your vision a reality?

Every gardener knows under the cloak of winter lies a miracle... a seed waiting to sprout, a bulb opening to light, a bud straining to unfurl. And the anticipation nurtures our dreams.

Barbara Winkler

Chapter 4

Window Shopping
(or "Size Matters!")

I love to browse plant farms and retail outlets, looking for new ideas and different plants. I even take pictures of displays. The tag on each plant provides critical information about it, such as when it blooms and whether it needs shade or full sun. It indicates the ideal climate zone and temperature range for the plant's survival. For my garden, certain plants will thrive, but others will not survive the cold of the winter or the heat of the summer. These are all critical bits of information to know about the plant. I call it "window shopping" research.

Knowing how tall a plant will grow is also essential. Plant tags usually mention the height and width of the mature plant, but people buying from local nurseries often overlook this. They place the plant in the wrong or inappropriate space for optimal growth. Homeowners often plant shrubs and trees too close to the house, causing them to quickly fill the space and crowd the structure.

You often see an area over-planted with large trees reaching thirty or forty feet, which creates deep shade over time.

This happens because many people buy their trees and shrubs when they are small and "cute," then plant them without regard to how they will mature. This is bad gardening. Size does matter to the experienced gardener.

What is the application to our lives? Do your research on each plant you buy. Then, you will understand what your choices might look like in the years to come. Life is fluid, but it's important to understand how choices develop into lifestyles, habits, and exposure to risk. I used to think and act like someone who was a risk-taker, but my natural inclination is to be very risk averse.

(Remember my favorite Latin phrase, "Above all else, do no harm?") In my earlier, more reckless years, my life was chaotic and stress-producing, not only for me but for my family, and especially my wife. She and I often talk about counting the cost. We can't see the future, but we can draw straight lines from now to the following year. Do your research and proceed with caution.

What kind of research (window shopping) do you like? How is that important to you?

What essential research do you need to start doing now?

My green thumb came only as a result of the mistakes I made while learning to see things from the plant's point of view.

H. Fred Ale

Chapter 5

Growing The Artist in You

I see myself as an artist in the dirt, experimenting with color, texture, height, and line of sight. I also look closely at other gardens and read gardening magazines for ideas to fold into my garden.

When I am in the waiting room for a doctor's appointment, I am probably the only man carefully going through Southern Living magazine. I have been known to quietly tear out the most interesting pages from magazines just to be sure I get the concept right. (My apologies to Dr. Lynch and his staff.)

Not everything I try works. When an experiment fails, I remind myself that nothing lasts forever. Experimentation allows me to be happily surprised, and often I am. My artist's palate includes soil, water, stone, wood, evergreens, deciduous plants, different leaf colors and textures, compact plant or airy form, low-growing or high-climbing vines, and a multitude of leaf shapes and sizes.

There is no end to the combinations that the artist gardener has at his disposal.

Art touches our souls. It's more visceral than something we can explain and is one of the most honest and unique ways we communicate. The true artist is able to express himself at the most elemental level. I love the surprises, new experiences, and fun that bring color and texture to life.

I express my love of art through gardening. People who have walked my garden confirm my artistic intent with their comments of delight.

How do you express yourself in what you do?

In what ways do you nurture your artistic desires?

Gardening is the art that uses flowers and plants as paint, and the soil and sky as canvas.

Elizabeth Murray

Chapter 6

Accepting Change and Making It Work for You

I must be willing to accept change in my garden. Some plants don't flourish where I first put them, and some visual effects I want to achieve just don't work. A hot and dry summer or severe winter will take its toll on plants and require rethinking those areas around the pond. It hurts to lose a plant I have been growing for three or four years; I almost go into mourning or a mild depression when that happens (yes, really).

Because of the changes, my garden will take on a new look over the years. Where there was speckled shade, there is now glaring sun, so I must create a new plan for that corner of the garden. Bright-colored annuals might work best for now, so I get on my knees and prepare the planting bed. I miss the shade I lost but can embrace the fresh colors and butterflies the new landscape will attract.

Life is a series of changes. I once heard a little boy say, "I don't ever want to grow up!" But he did grow up, bought a truck, and moved away from his mother and me. Change comes to all of us. How we see change in our mind's eye is important because it determines how we manage it.

Yes, change can be scary, so we need to trust in something far greater than ourselves to walk us through it with less pain and fear. When that beautifully shaped tree gets blown over in the storm, we can trust that this new space—now open and brightened by sunlight—can be used to plant something new and special. That space may now attract butterflies and hummingbirds, making the change meaningful.

What changes in your life's garden have been the most significant for you?

All through the long winter, I dream of my garden. On the first day of spring, I dig my fingers deep into the soft earth. I can feel its energy, and my spirits soar.

Helen Hayes

Chapter 7

Blind Faith, Mud, and Mess

Several years ago, I looked at what I had planted in the garden and found myself at a loss. I loved how things looked; it was a joy to do my part, but I knew there was more to be done. I couldn't go much further with the way things were. In the middle of the garden was an old rustic wooden deck and a concrete pad originally installed for a hot tub. I had planted Grace Garden around these structures but knew they had to go.

I had a strong feeling about this but had no notion of anything beyond that. So, I asked a contractor to remove them. It was no small job, and the scar left after their removal was ugly. My wife went along with the plan with reservations. I think she knew it would take a long time for a new structure to fill the void and that I had limited time and energy to make anything happen quickly. It took two years before I knew with certainty what would go in that empty space.

I began to plan and scheme what a water feature would look like and calculate the installation cost.

Looking back on those two years, I can't imagine coming up with anything else that would have worked as well in that location. The new vision of a pond became a reality and is now the primary focus of Grace Garden. When guests walk into our home, the pond is one of the first things they see as they look toward the rear of the house.

I hired an experienced rock worker to do the heavy work of digging and laying out the rock. He explained it this way: "If you are a gardener, water is just another medium to use, like any artist."

I think God must have put us together.

Sometimes, we have a strong sense that something needs to change. As a man of faith, I know how the Holy Spirit speaks to me. Walking by faith sometimes means trusting dramatic change needs to happen, even when we can't see the outcome. In this instance, a scar of mud, weeds, and lots of questions were all part of creating a one-of-a-kind water feature that became the center point of Grace Garden. What a difference it made!

What acts of blind faith have you experienced in the past?

What act of faith do you face right now?

For we walk by faith, not by sight.

The Apostle Paul (2 Corinthians 5:7 ESV)

Chapter 8

Hold Out for The Best Fit

I am a firm believer in working toward per-
fection. I will never reach that goal, but I believe
we are blessed when we do our best in whatever
activity in which we engage. I'm not content to
settle for second best. As a gardener, if some plants
don't seem to fit after a few months or years, I
change them out with something more suitable.
Seeking the best for my garden means having a
long-term view of things, which is a constant issue
for the gardener. Many people plant small trees
or shrubs that no longer fit the space when fully
grown. In their mind, they will be long gone before
a problem emerges. That attitude doesn't sound
like a gardener to me. I'm a guy who works hard
to find the right size plant for the right location.

In life, seeking the best also requires a long-
term view of things. It also means being comfort-
able with delayed gratification. In the garden, it
might mean putting up with a small, gangly plant
until it comes into its own—much like the growth
process during our teenage years. Often, a spot

in the garden is bare and lonely, with nothing of interest, until the right plant comes along.

Knowledge, experience, and some hard-earned wisdom have shown me that some things are worth waiting for.

———————————————————

What should you hold out for in your life's garden right now?

Adopt the pace of nature: her secret is patience.
Ralph Waldo Emerson

Chapter 9

All the Days
Ordained for Me

All the days ordained for me were written in your book before one of them came to be. (Psalm 139:16)

Everything that lives has a life cycle. We all emerge from a seed, grow, mature, decline, and finally die. Scripture puts it well, as the Hebrew Psalmist laments in Psalms 103:15 ESV: *As for man, his days are like grass; he flourishes like a flower of the field.* A little-known aspect of gardening is the grief and disappointment we feel when what we plant and nurture fails at some point.

I use grasses to create movement in the wind or form soft edges around sharp corners. Over time, some grasses do not re-emerge in the spring as I had hoped. I must find something else for its place or buy new grasses to replace it. Perennials are like that, too. Over the years, most become spent and need to be replaced.

So much depends on your perspective. Understanding plant life cycles is crucial if you garden with a five-to-ten-year view like me. It also allows me to appreciate the moments when everything seems to work together. The garden is gracious, allowing me to experience the complete life cycles of many of its congregation. A quiet, calming sense of peace comes over me when I walk into a well-established garden, like walking through a grand cathedral. I fall silent as if on hallowed ground, and, indeed, it is. To me, the garden is a temple of our human efforts to glorify God's creation. I know that plants have come and gone from a garden space that I have never seen. Likewise, plants unknown to me will appear in the future that I will never see. *Lord, our Lord, how majestic is your name in all the earth! (Psalms 8:1)*

How does our mortality impact us in what we do, how we spend our time, and the people we let into our lives?

How does our mortality affect the people we have become?

Nature is man's teacher. She unfolds her treasures to his search, unseals his eye, illumes his mind, and purifies his heart; an influence breathes from all the sights and sounds of her existence.

Alfred Billings Street

Chapter 10

Resistance Builds Strength

A gardening article I read some time ago stated that when you stake a tree, for a time, you make a weak stalk even weaker. At first, that didn't make sense. However, as time goes by, if the plant is forced to contend with shifting winds, the cells of the stalk become stronger, and the plant stands straighter on its own. This applies to other areas of life as well. Physical trainers at my gym will tell you the same thing: resistance builds strength.

When difficult times come, and we resist the push and pull of circumstances, we can become stronger. As a gardener, I say: "Don't be concerned about the winds that shake up our lives." We can choose to allow them to build strength and resilience in us. A small tree has to be buffeted around to grow a strong stem and a solid core. We also need wind and storms to give us resilience. If we shelter ourselves, our children, or those around us, we take away their ability to stand tall and straight.

I undertook an intervention with a small tree I planted. I dug around it and moved the whole ball of roots to straighten it. It took a radical reorientation of the entire plant, but my tree is now growing straight and tall. It finally flourished after all that digging. The wind still batters it, but my tree grows stronger as it resists.

How have you been buffeted by life's winds?

What hidden strengths did you discover in yourself during the wind and storms?

What encouragement can you give to someone facing strong headwinds?

The history of liberty is a history of resistance.
Woodrow Wilson

Chapter 11

Weed 'Em When
You Find 'Em

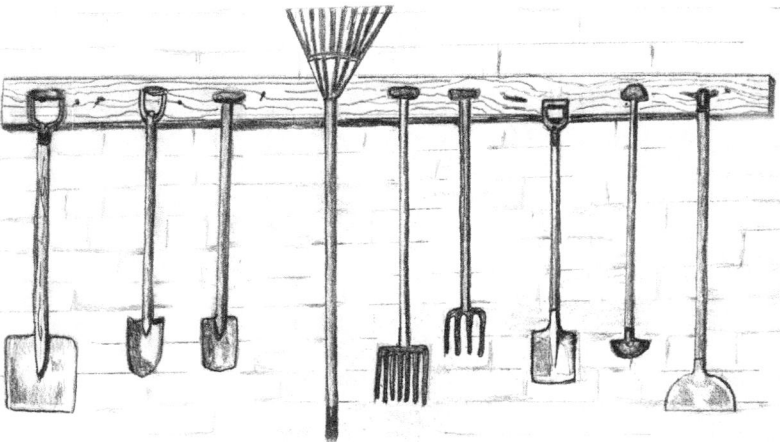

When I go out to work in my garden, I know a portion of my time will be spent weeding. I'm a little ADD, which means I'm easily (and often) distracted. It's possible I won't get back to the area where I am working anytime soon, so when moving plants around (shorter to the front, taller to the back), I weed at the same time. I also do this to conserve energy because of a limiting health issue. I must work in short spurts, but it seems to be paying off. A recent visitor commented on how clean the beds seemed. I didn't explain–just beamed and said, "Thank you."

So, what is the broader lesson?

Our lives are full of things that, if unattended, distract us, consume our time, overwhelm us, and seem to be a constant presence in our lives, like weeds. I often envision myself standing in the middle of my life's garden, and when I find a weed, I pull it up. My suggestion is to pull those weeds when and where you find them. Finding them isn't usually the problem. It's getting past the fear, pain, or whatever else is holding you back from grabbing the little rascals at the root line and pulling.

Let's take the metaphor one more step. Sometimes, we have habits and behaviors that require us to pull up the weeds with a lot of force. Other times, it's smaller issues in our lives, and it just takes a little gentle wiggling of the wrist to release those weeds. Let nothing hold you back.

Weed 'em when you find 'em, so you can pursue the creation of your life's garden as God intended.

Do you need to do any "weeding" in your life's garden?

Shall I not rejoice also at the abundance of the weeds whose seeds are the granary of the birds?

Henry David Thoreau

Chapter 12

Plant Them Where
They Can Bloom Best

I move plants around a lot. I joke that if they don't perform well, they are cast out. No grace from this gardener. That might be an overstatement, but I'm diligent about finding the right location for my plants. If they aren't thriving, I research where they might grow best, then find a spot in the garden that is better suited for them. Several plants in my garden did not belong where I first planted them, so I found a little spot where they could recover and grow stronger. Later, I found with the right amount of light and shade, the plants flourished. I told a neighbor a while back that one of his shrubs really loved the corner where he planted it. I have seen it many times in my own garden: when the plant finds its sweet spot, it just looks happy, healthy, and content. And it grows.

I used to believe in the old saying, "Bloom where you are planted." It suggests that if you find yourself in a difficult situation, suck it up, do your very best, and the reward will eventually come your way. I have learned so much as I have grown older and spent time in my garden. I now encourage people to learn as much as they can about who they are and what they do best. Then, find a place to plant themselves where they will succeed.

I think God is asking something bigger of us than simply to bloom where we are planted. He has made us all unique, with special attributes and abilities to do the things He has already set aside for us. One of the great adventures in living is searching out God's purpose for us. We have many fine tools for that, including coaches and counselors. Instead of "bloom where you are planted," I say, "plant yourself where you bloom!" Joy, happiness, and influence will be yours.

You will feel successful in life, whatever the outcome. I now work hard to place my plants where they will bloom best.

What does it feel like in your mind to be planted where you cannot bloom?

Where do you believe you bloom best?

There is no gardening without humility. Nature is constantly sending even its oldest scholars to the bottom of the class for some egregious blunder.

Alfred Austin

Chapter 13

A Time for Everything

I grew up In the Midwest, with four seasons, but the winters lingered far too long, and summers were oh, so short. When I moved to Oklahoma over thirty years ago, I was surprised to discover that Spring comes early and warm late Fall days last well into November.

In my gardening world, the changing seasons mean new phases of rebirth, growth, and dying. I appreciate each season for what it is and how it changes my view of the garden. I now appreciate the previous season and anticipate the next one. The changing seasons also affect my gardening activities. In the spring and summer, I make notes about certain areas of the garden where I want to move plants in the fall. In the winter, I focus on mulch, prepping beds for the new growth ahead, pruning back shrubs and small trees, and clipping the grasses low. Winter is also my time for planning ahead, envisioning what things will look like in the summer, and listing the chores to make it happen.

We often describe the phases of our own lives as seasons. Ecclesiastes 3 describes a time for everything. The older I get, the more I understand this. I often hear people lamenting about being in the winter of their lives; the spring of youth is over, and the heat of summer in early adulthood is gone. In the fall, we reminisce about the vigor we once had, sometimes injuring ourselves as we try to recapture it. As we move into our later years—the winter of our lives—we ask, "What can I possibly do now except wait for death to overcome me?"

In my garden, winter is often the busiest time. Planning, seeking out new plants, designing and repairing the plumbing or electrical utilities that support the garden all require urgent attention. I see my own later years in the same way. This is when I must plan and envision what things may look like in the years to come, even the ones I may never see. This is not a time to fear or withdraw from the garden. It is a time to prepare for the generation to come and celebrate the future. There is so much to do, and I may not get it all done.

If you are in the fall or winter of your life, what should you be busy doing right now?

What resources do you have for accomplishing tasks in the winter of your life?

"In the midst of winter, I finally learned that within me there lay an invincible summer."

Albert Camus

Chapter 14

A Metaphor for Life

Now the Lord God had planted a garden in the
east, in Eden, and there He put the man He formed.
(Genesis 2:8)

The Garden of Eden is often referred to as an earthly paradise created by God. His purpose was to have an intimate relationship with Man, whom He fashioned out of the earth. The Biblical account goes on to describe how God made Woman from Man. Together, they enjoyed total freedom and complete communion with God. Living close to nature in my younger years and now in my garden, I can say without a doubt that I have communion with God. In rare moments, it is complete communion. I tend to the small tasks in my garden, bound in by fence and shrub, totally safe and secure, much like Adam.

And I have also eaten of the fruit of the tree of knowledge and have suffered for it. I pursued directions I thought were true in my own mind, and yet, over time, they proved false. When I finally surrendered my life to God, I found the safety and peace cultivated in that Garden so long ago.

The Garden of Eden is a metaphor for my life. Even in the midst of safety and security, Evil creeps about, so innocent in its suggestions and entice-ments. The Fall of Man is yet another metaphor for the Fall of Me. For that reason, I am grateful for the Word I received years ago to "just dig." Digging in the dirt has brought me closer to God.

What new metaphor would you like to create in your life?

No occupation is so delightful to me as the culture of the earth and no culture comparable to that of the garden.

Thomas Jefferson

Chapter 15

One Final Note

Reflecting on the lessons learned from the garden I was called to tend, I have one last question: Were those years in the garden only for life lessons, or is there something more? I am beginning to see another storyline here. Scripture says: *The Lord will fulfill his purpose for me* (Psalms 138:8) and *You have searched me, Lord and you know me.* (Psalms 139:1) And later, *For you formed my inward parts; you knitted me together in my mother's womb. I praise you, for I am fearfully and wonderfully made.* (Psalms 139:13–14 ESV)

How I tend my garden reveals more of who I am. This is God's gift to me. He has given me living brushes of color and life to express myself as He has made me. The garden is an expression of who I am. In addition to important life lessons, God wanted to underscore that He loves me just as I am. How universal and yet how intimate God can be at the same time!

Remarkable.

My final word to you: Plant yourself where you bloom!

Were those years in the garden only for life lessons, or is there something more?

The real voyage of discovery consists not in seeking new landscapes, but in having new eyes.

Marcel Proust

About the Author

Rod was born and raised in northern Iowa, where his childhood home overlooked a forested city park. In this place, he fostered a deep relationship with both nature and God. He graduated from the University of Iowa with degrees in business and health administration. His first job after graduation took him to Oklahoma. At age 51, Rod suffered a severe heart attack and took up gardening during his long recovery. His garden was not only therapy but also allowed him to express his creativity. Rod often says that God can use all of our past experiences to create a testimony for His Glory. Rod and his wife Charlene raised their three children in Tulsa, where they still live.

Notes

Made in the USA
Monee, IL
07 September 2024

64724808R00062